fences *and* hedges

and other garden dividers

Richard Bird

photography by **Stephen Robson**

RYLAND
PETERS
& SMALL
LONDON · NEW YORK

First published in the USA in 1998.

This new edition published in 2002 by
Ryland Peters & Small, Inc.
519 Broadway
5th Floor
New York, NY 10012
www.rylandpeters.com
10 9 8 7 6 5 4 3 2

Text © Richard Bird 1998, 2002
Design, illustrations and photographs
© Ryland Peters & Small 1998, 2002

ISBN 1 84172 312 6

Printed in China
10 9 8 7 6 5 4 3 2

Designer **Luana Gobbo**
Senior editor **Henrietta Heald**
Production **Martin Croshaw**
Art director **Gabriella Le Grazie**
Publishing director **Alison Starling**

Consultant **David Grist**

The 1998 edition of this book was
designed by **Liz Brown**, **Vicky Holmes**,
and **Mark Latter**, and edited by
Sarah Polden and Ann Snyder.

contents

All gardens have to have boundaries, something to limit them and to prevent them from merging with the neighboring yard. In the past, boundaries were purely protective, to keep animals and undesirable visitors out. Today, they still perform this function, but they also have other purposes, including preserving privacy and reducing the interference of outside noise.

Within the garden, boundaries can be used to divide or screen the space or to delineate different areas. Screens can hide trash cans or they can create a sense of mystery, guarding part of the garden from the viewer who feels compelled to investigate; similarly, an archway can mark two different areas of the garden, allowing only a glimpse of one from the other, while pathways might join two areas or separate them, creating a boundary between the lawn and a flower bed. Internal boundaries can be permanent, such as a stream, or temporary, such as the summer display of tall, bright annuals.

As well as having a practical function, boundaries are excellent for decorating the garden. They can be decorative in their own right, seen in a beautiful hedge or striking pleached trees, or they can be used to support and protect plants, a wall, fence, or trellis covered by a scrambling climber. Boundaries create a backdrop against which the rest of the garden can be seen, setting the tone for the design and the planting.

In their various ways, boundaries are a very important part of any garden, and in this book we offer practical and imaginative suggestions for making the most of your needs and desires.

above Use the shelter and warmth offered by a wall to grow tender plants such as grapes. They will respond well and are an unusual and appealing sight.

left A traditional, period house can take exuberant growth—but not at the cost of light. Allow climbers to grow around windows but not over or through them!

below A bold plaque, effective tile work, and lush foliage create a well-balanced design. Look for garden ornaments that reflect the age and style of your home.

walls are the most solid of garden boundaries and usually mark

the perimeter of the garden, be it the house or garden wall. They very much set the tone of the whole planting display, offering a versatile canvas for abundant climbers, restrained architectural displays, mounted containers, or fountains and ornaments. A plain wall can be covered with growth, an attractive one highlighted by foliage and flowers.

above Seasonal interest is a priority for walls that are so much on view. The leaves of this climber are turning for their autumn show.

right If your garden is large enough to offer a vista, then take advantage of it. Here, the very absence of part of the wall leads the eye to the next point of interest.

above Fruit trees bring homey comfort to a garden and a trained plant adds order without formality.

left Roses, rightly a constant favorite, give a glorious performance when they have a large wall to cover.

house wall

ONE OF THE MOST satisfying aspects of gardening is to integrate the house successfully into the overall garden design. The use of climbers and wall shrubs is a very effective way of achieving this. Climbing plants not only help to unify the scheme but they can also transform a house, softening lines and bringing seasonal interest. Fragrant climbers, such as the rose 'Mme Alfred Carrière', grown around windows can fill a room with perfume during the summer.

materials & equipment

30 vine eyes
30 ft (9 m) galvanized wire
1 bucket well-rotted organic material
1 *Rosa* 'Mme Alfred Carrière'
or similar climber
4 bamboo stakes
plant ties

hammer, pliers, pruners, spade

garden wall

GARDEN WALLS come in all shapes and sizes, some beautiful in their own right, others less attractive. Plants can be used in a variety of ways either to enhance the wall's appearance or to conceal it. Walls can be the perfect visual foil for plants, supplying a neutral backdrop for informal and formal displays alike. They also provide physical support and protection. Where space is limited, walls can carry containers filled with seasonal plants or work with an elegantly planted raised bed.

materials & equipment

wall support
3 vine eyes for the first yd (m) then
2 per yd (m)
galvanized wire to cover the length of the
wall plus 12 in (30 cm) for securing,
multiplied by the number of tiers required

drill, hammer, pliers

planting
3 buckets of organic material per sq yd (sq m)
plants (*see plan opposite*)
3 3-ft (1-m) bamboo stakes for the wall plants
plant ties

fork, spade, rake, trowel, pruners,
watering can

fruit wall

WALLS CAN SUSTAIN plants that are both productive and decorative:
all manner of fruits can be trained to take on elegant, geometric shapes.
Apples and pears can be grown as cordons and, as here, espaliers, while
plums, peaches, and nectarines are excellent for fan training. These
traditional forms have graced walls for centuries. Figs, grapes, passion
fruit, and all manner of currants and berries can also be grown against
a wall that will provide warmth and protection to the growing plant.

materials & equipment

9 vine eyes
30 ft (9 m) galvanized wire
1 1-year-old pear tree
3 bamboo stakes
plant ties
1 bucket of well-rotted organic material

hammer, pliers, pruners, spade

retaining wall

SLOPES IN A GARDEN can cause problems. One solution is to make a virtue of them by dividing the garden into different levels using retaining walls. These can be planted up in various ways, from grass to highly ornamental displays, and the surface of the walls can become a decorative feature in its own right. If you live in an area where the ground freezes, you will have to make modifications to ensure the stability of your wall. Consult a local professional for advice.

materials & equipment

for every 8 ft (2.5 m) of wall
concrete
mortar
random-size stone blocks,
about 6 cu ft (0.1 cu m)
2 terra-cotta drainage pipes

for the bed
coarse gravel or small rocks
good topsoil or well-rotted
organic material

mason's trowel, shovel, spade, wheelbarrow

Please note: This project is a bit more complicated than others in the book. Unless you have previous experience with masonry, it is best to consult a professional, using these plans as a guide.

wall cascade

WALLS CAN enhance garden design, especially when decorated with plants, containers, or a water feature. The slate "steps" in this garden have been drilled with outlet holes, but a simple hollow, as used in the project, is just as effective. Plan the feature in advance, finalizing all measurements and proportions. If you live in an area where the ground freezes, you will have to make modifications to ensure the stability of the walls and the pool. Consult a local professional for advice.

materials & equipment

gravel
concrete
6 x 6 10/10 reinforcing mesh
to cover 24 x 72 in (60 x 180 cm)
5 slabs of slate or cast concrete, slightly concave
brick
mortar
about 16 concrete capstones 10 x 12 in (25 x 30 cm)
flexible pond liner
2 sheets landscape fabric
submersible pump and fittings (choose a pump
that can handle the volume of the pool and
the height of the cascade)
½ in (1 cm) PVC pipe, about 7 ft (2.2 m)

*Please note: This project is a bit more complicated than others in
the book. Unless you have previous experience with masonry, it is
best to consult a professional, using these plans as a guide.*

above Holly (*Ilex aquifolium*) produces an impenetrable, fine-looking hedge with its dark green, shiny leaves.

above Archways in hedges present inviting glimpses of what lies beyond, enticing the viewer to walk through.

above Yew (*Taxus baccata*) creates a wonderfully solid, uniform hedge that makes a perfect backdrop.

hedges can provide far more than a merely functional boundary between two properties; they can be decorative features in their own right. They present the possibility of using a wide range of textures and colors as well as a variety of shapes to enliven a garden.

left and above Compact-growing boxwood (*Buxus sempervirens*) is the perfect shrub for low hedging. It is particularly suitable for creating parterres, where hedges are laid out in formal patterns and filled in with contrasting plants. Such geometric designs can work well even in a small garden, adding classical order. Patience is required when growing box as it makes slow progress; however, once established, it is a reliable, hardy, long-lived plant.

above Yew is a very sculptural material that can be used very successfully to create all manner of topiary. Here, the elegant birds sit above the hedge for greatest impact.

above The versatility of close-growing hedging plants such as yew allows for practical garden features to be created from plants, adding to their charm and interest.

left and below A wide range of shrubs can be used to create informal hedges. These are left largely untrimmed, giving any flower buds a chance to open. Roses, in particular *Rosa rugosa*, are good shrubs to use but other fine flowering hedges are made from lilac, lavender, and hebe. They bring abundance to a garden and often delicious fragrance.

below To relieve the uniformity of a formal hedge, a flowering plant such as this rose can be used to break up the line and color.

formal hedge

FORMAL HEDGES add elegance to a garden, their clean lines bringing an architectural quality to the design. Most formal hedging is relatively slow growing and so does not need much trimming to keep it looking good. Once established, a dense hedge will form an effective windbreak and bring privacy and security to the garden. Yew springs to mind most often when formal hedges are considered, but this beech gives glorious autumn color after the spring greenery.

materials & equipment

1 bucket of organic material per plant
3 beech saplings for the first yd (m), then 2 per yd (m)
1 stake at either end of the planting, then 1 stake for
every 6 ft (1.8 m) of hedging
plastic windbreak netting

club hammer, fork, garden line, hoe or rake,
measuring tape, spade

informal hedge

NEATLY CLIPPED hedges are an attractive sight but the other side of the coin also has enormous appeal. Informal hedges allow shrubs the freedom to grow and flower and fruit at will. What they lose in neatness and order they gain in variety and cheerfulness. They bring abundance to a garden scene and blend into a free-growing scheme. The added benefit is that informal hedges do not have to be regularly pruned; they will benefit from such maintenance but can look the part without.

materials & equipment

1 bag of mulch per 7 ft (2.2 m)
1 *Rosa rugosa* plant per 4 ft (1.2 m)

fork, spade, hoe or rake, garden line,
watering can, pruners

hedge feature

HEDGES CAN BE integrated completely into the garden scene by incorporating a built-in feature that is both practical and decorative. Here, a niche has been carved into a hornbeam hedge to create a secluded and quiet spot for relaxing and contemplating the garden. It is best if the arbor is constructed when the hedge is first laid, for although it is possible to create such a recess by pruning away growth, it will take some years for the cut areas to green up.

materials & equipment

4 hornbeam (*Carpinus betulus*) or beech saplings per yd (m)
for each row of the hedge
2 buckets of well-rotted organic material per yd (m)
windbreak netting
1 post per 3 ft (1 m) of netting
staples or string
1 garden bench

hammer, pruners, spade

low hedge

LOW HEDGES are an ideal way of creating internal divisions
in addition to edging beds. They form a clean line between different
areas of the garden, often, as here, holding back the abundant growth
of a border from a grass path or lawn. The hedge has been further
defined by a rim of charming purple-leafed pansies. Hedges such as
these look best if they are kept trimmed, but slow-growing plants
like boxwood require little attention to produce a neat finish.

materials & equipment

12 *Buxus sempervirens* plants per yd (m)
12 pansy plants per yd (m)
plants for the enclosed bed (*see plan opposite*)

fork, hand-fork, hedge clippers, pruners, spade, trowel

pruning template
2 18 x 18-in (45 x 45-cm) pieces of plywood
1 ball of string

fences
offer the gardener many options. They can provide a highly rustic mood or take on an elegant geometric quality. Trellis and woven panels come into their own where an internal boundary is needed, and all combine well with plants, be they adjacent beds or scrambling climbers.

above Fences can form a boundary without obscuring the view. Where security is not a problem, a stylish, low, minimalist fence is all that is needed to end a garden.

right The position, size, and all-important design of a gate are significant factors. A double gateway allows more room for creativity.

above A trellis is well suited to making garden "rooms." It gives height and can extend across a wide area, enclose a corner, or emphasize a design. And it can become home for climbers—from honeysuckle to roses, jasmine to clematis—or a bold display of nasturtiums.

above A classic feature of many country homes is the crisp, white picket fence, a traditional boundary that justifies its popularity. Fresh, bright posts deserve to be complemented by colorful cottage-garden flowers. Natural wood has a more restrained character while a green or blue stain makes an eye-catching statement.

right This beautiful fence seems to glow from a shady corner. Beyond, tall fronds of lavender echo the blueness of the shade.

above Rustic trellis adds informality with its bark-covered finish and suitability for witty, asymmetrical designs. An excellent screen.

right There are few garden features that add a more rural note than a woven "wattle" panel. Originally used by farmers to contain livestock, they now hide unsightly parts of the garden, protect young trees, and create tantalizing passageways to explore.

49

picket fence

SMALL FLAT OR POINTED pickets are easy to construct providing the fence is well planned; a sabersaw is useful for more ornate finials. The height of the fence and the distance between the posts is up to you. The rails are usually placed about a quarter of the way from the top and the bottom. The pickets are usually spaced about 3 in (7.5 cm) apart. In areas where the ground freezes, posts should be set 6 in (15 cm) below the frost line. Consult a local professional for advice.

materials & equipment

for each section of fence you need the following items:

gravel or prepared concrete

2 pressure-treated posts 3½ x 3½ in [4 x 4]
(10 x 10 cm)

pickets ¾ x 2½ in [1 x 3] (1 x 7.5 cm)

2 rails 1½ x 3½ in [2 x 4] (4 x 8 cm)

galvanized nails

trellis

FREESTANDING TRELLIS is perfect for supporting climbing plants in their numerous forms, creating a dense screen of foliage and color. This versatile garden structure can also be incorporated into arches, pergolas, or arbors, providing a foothold for plants while allowing light and air through. It must be bedded firmly in the ground. If you live in an area where the ground freezes, aim to set your posts 6 in (150 mm) below the frost line. Consult a local professional for advice.

materials & equipment

ready-made lattice panels, usually sold in 4 x 8 ft
(1.2 x 2.4 m) sheets

¾ x 1½ in [1 x 2] (5 x 5 cm) lumber for attaching
lattice panel to post

pressure-treated posts 4 x 4 in (10 x 10 cm), sized
to accommodate the lattice panels and the post hole

post-hole digger

1 finial per post

gravel or prepared concrete for each hole

galvanized nails

plant ties

clematis, honeysuckle, roses, or other climbing
plants

hammer, level, measuring tape, spade

wattle panels

TO PROVIDE AN attractive temporary screen, there is nothing better than wattle panels. They have a rustic appearance that is effective in less formal settings, and they also work well in modern schemes. Their original purpose was to protect and fence in sheep; they can serve a similar function today, keeping pets in or out of a particular part of the garden. Wattle fences do not last many years, but providing they are not unstable or dangerous, aged panels can be picturesque.

materials & equipment

6 ft (1.8 m) posts: 2 for the first panel,
then 1 per panel
1 wattle panel 6 x 4 ft (1.8 x 1.2 m)
for each 6 ft (1.8 m) run
galvanized wire
level, pliers, spade

rustic trellis

THE WOOD USED for this trellis has not been machined,
making it pleasingly irregular in thickness and shape. The structure
can be covered with plants, but if a more restrained covering is
preferred, rustic trellis is ideal because it is attractive in its own right.
The trellis is available ready-made but it is very simple to construct—
requiring no advanced carpentry skills—and making your own
allows you to tailor the design to your needs.

materials & equipment

4 in (10 cm) galvanized nails
exterior-grade wood preservative
chisel, hammer, level, measuring tape
saw, shovel, spade

for each 6 ft (1.8 m) section of trellis
gravel or prepared concrete for each post hole
uprights: 1 cedar pole 8-ft (2.5-m) long x 4–5 in (10–25 cm)
across (1 pole for each section, plus 1 extra)
crossbars: 2 cedar poles 8-ft (2.5-m) long x 3–4 in (8–10 cm)
struts: 3 cedar poles 3-ft (90-cm) long x 3–4 in (8–10 cm)

gateway

AN INTERNAL GATEWAY can be imaginatively integrated into a garden design, marking the boundary of a separate area and framing what lies beyond. The length of the uprights used in this project depends on the desired height of the finished gateway—and the spacing between posts will vary depending on the size of your arches and the desired distance between them. The length, quantity, and spacing of the pickets will also be determined by the height of the finished gateway.

materials & equipment

1 bucket gravel for each hole

arches
2 8-ft (2.5-m) lengths of 1 x 8-in (2.5 x 20-cm) lumber for curved tops
4 6½-ft (2-m) lengths of 1 x 6-in (2.5 x 15-cm) lumber for uprights
130 ft (39 m) of ¾ x 1½-in (2 x 3 cm) lumber for inside batten and horizontal lattice
110 ft (33 m) of ½ x ¾-in (1 x 2-cm) lumber for vertical lattice
1¼-in (3-cm) galvanized nails

gate
1 x 2-in (2.5 x 5-cm) lumber for pickets
1 x 3-in (2.5 x 7.5-cm) lumber for rails
1½-in (3-cm) galvanized nails
2 strap hinges
gate latch
screws

large sheet of paper, measuring tape, pencil, chisel, hammer, saw, shovel, spade, square, wood glue, paintbrushes, primer, paint or stain

above A trellis-pillar gives distinction to the corner of a garden shelter; the roses draw you closer.

above Shapes and textures work together in a stepped path, given softness by the pergola-style arches.

above A stream marks a clear divide in a garden, whether architectural and orderly or informal and lush.

decorative dividers are the screens

and edgings, boundaries and barriers that do not reflect standard forms. Pleached trees can march across a garden or a fragrant row of sweet peas can delineate a border. A rose-covered archway can curve over a path or a line of sunflowers can bring delight one year, to be replaced by runner beans the next. Illusion even plays its part, mirrors revealing a scene that is not there.

above Strongly trained and structured fruit trees can form a decorative screen.

right Smaller touches can make a surprising difference in the garden. Edging hurdles bring a note of order to abundant growth.

above The curious structure of pleached trees is best seen during the winter when their highly pruned, twiggy branches stand out starkly.

left An orchard in bloom. The row of trees is grouped with lines of irises and rose bushes and a swathe of tulips. The spring flowers bring gaiety to the order.

below Given space, a single pleached tree can form a boundary. Here, ranked specimens are both strange and impressive.

plant screen

WHILE BOUNDARIES that mark the perimeters of a garden are likely to be permanent, there is no reason why those within the garden should not change from time to time, both in location and in composition. Unsupported tall annuals such as sunflowers are perfect for such a divider. Their flowers add a touch of brightness and gaiety to the boundary while their foliage provides a more solid screen. Grow plants from seed for an inexpensive display that can change yearly.

materials & equipment

enough seed to produce at least
20 *Helianthus annuus* 'Velvet Queen'
enough seed to produce at least
20 *Tropaeolum majus* (nasturtiums)
40 pots
potting soil

rose arch

ARCHES CAN BE put to very good use in the garden, dividing one area from another, but their greatest asset is that they are ideal for growing climbers. Arches entice you to pass through and your reward with this example would be the fragrance of the rambling rose. Wooden archways can be made from scratch but a variety of elegant metal and wooden frames are readily available in easy-assemble kit form, so any garden can be given a passageway and a home for delightful climbers.

materials & equipment

gravel or concrete (for securing the arch to the ground)
2 *Rosa* 'Adélaïde d'Orléans' plants
well-rotted manure or compost for each plant

fork, level, plant ties, pruners, shovel, spade

pleached trees

USUALLY ASSOCIATED WITH large formal grounds, a boundary or
avenue of pleached trees works well in a smaller garden because the
trees are kept clipped. Use strong posts that can be sunk 24 in (60 cm)
into the ground; the above-ground part of each post should be as high
as the top tier of the finished boundary. The height and length of the
border can vary to fit the situation and the type of tree. Suitable choices
include crabapple, hornbeam, and linden, which is used in this project.

materials & equipment

supporting framework for each section
posts, about 4–5 in (10–12.5 cm) diameter
(one for each tree)
galvanized wire
galvanized staples

hammer, level, spade, tape measure

plants
1 bucket organic material per tree
3- or 4-year-old trees, such as *Tilia platyphyllos*

sweet-pea divider

UNLIKE FIXED FEATURES such as hedges and walls, temporary dividers mean the gardener can move elements around and alter the shape of a design. Such temporary displays can also be used as screens while a permanent feature, such as a tree, is growing. Many plants can be used to make a divider; brightly colored summer flowers such as sweet peas can completely change the appearance of a garden, proving so successful that they become an annual feature.

materials & equipment

for a 10-ft (3-m) run
2 wooden stakes
ball of string
3 8-ft (2.5-m) poles
12 pea stakes (any leafless branch with plenty of twiggy growth)
1 bag organic material

mallet, pruners, rake, spade or fork, trowel

plants
Lathyrus odoratus (12 plants or a packet of seed)

miniature hurdles

DECORATIVE EDGING adds a finishing touch to borders and paths, defining the boundary between one area and another. An edging can also serve other, practical functions; here, the charming miniature hurdles, or fences, hold back the plants from the lawn and deter pets from running into the border. Canes can do the same job but are far less attractive. These decorative hurdles can be bought, or they are simple to make—an excellent project for the novice carpenter.

materials & equipment

For each hurdle
2 uprights 9 in (23 cm) long and 2 in (5 cm) across
5 crossbars 16 in (40 cm) long and 1 in (2.5 cm) across
3 braces 8 in (20 cm) long and 1 in (2.5 cm) across
galvanized nails
exterior-grade wood preservative

chisel, drill, hammer, sharp knife

trompe l'oeil

A CAREFULLY DEVISED trompe l'oeil gives the impression that
a garden continues beyond its fixed perimeters. A scene reflecting the
style and scale of your garden can be painted in durable paints—or a
mirror can be used, as here, to reflect parts of the real garden. For the
trellis, choose a weather-resistant wood, such as cedar or redwood.

*Please note: This project is a bit more complex that others in the book. Unless you
have previous experience with masonry and construction, it is best to consult a
professional, using these plans as a guide and an inspiration. Where dimensions
are not specified, they are determined by the size of the finished project.*

materials & equipment

mirror, sized to fit behind the center arch
hardware, suitable for attaching the mirror to the wall
cardboard
particle board
2 x 4-in (5 x 10-cm) lumber
prepared concrete
bricks
prepared mortar

trellis
2 x 6-in (5 x 15-cm) lumber
2 x 8-in (5 x 20-cm) lumber
2 x 4-in (5 x 10-cm) lumber
½-in (1-cm) diameter wooden dowel
¾ x 1½-in (2 x 4-cm) lattice
¾-in (2-cm) galvanized nails

large sheet of paper, pencil, string, tape measure, masking tape, spade, shovel,
band saw, bricklayer's trowel, builder's square, chisel, drill, hammer, level,
exterior-grade wood stain, paintbrush, wood glue

basic techniques

LIVING BOUNDARIES

SOIL PREPARATION

To get the best results from any plants, it is essential to prepare the ground thoroughly. Remove all perennial weeds either by digging and removing by hand or by using weed killers, carefully following the instructions for the product. If possible, leave the ground fallow for at least six months and remove any weeds that reappear. Prepare the soil in the early fall and plant in the spring.

digging

Dig the ground; if it is heavy, break up the soil below the top layer with a fork and work organic material into this. The addition of large quantities of organic material will improve the structure of the soil, will provide nutrients for the plants, and will help preserve moisture around the roots of the plants. Methodical double digging can pay great dividends for the future health and productivity of a bed, so is well worth the effort involved. Do not dig if the ground is wet and, once the double digging has been

completed, leave the area to allow winter frosts and rain to break down the soil and kill pests. Avoid walking on the area during this time because it can compact the soil.

2 *Work the trench for a further 12 in (30 cm) and add organic material. Dig out the next trench and use the earth to fill the first.*

3 *As before, work through the layer below, breaking up the ground with a fork and adding organic material. Continue to work in this way.*

double digging
1 *Dig a trench, 12–18 in (30–45 cm) wide and 12 in (30 cm) deep. Save the removed earth.*

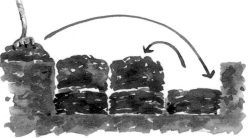

4 *When you have reached the end of the border, fill the final trench with the earth removed from the first trench.*

drainage

Other than those native to marshland or water, plants do not like to be waterlogged, so, if water remains in the soil, it is important to install some form of drainage system such as digging a ditch or laying drainage tile. The most appropriate approach will depend on the site and the plants. Sand should also be added to the soil to help water seep through.

drainage systems
An effective drainage system can be created by digging a hole 4–6 ft (1.2–1.8 m) deep and adding broken stones topped with good-quality soil.

A shallower hole of 24 in (60 cm) will be effective if drainage tile is used in a herringbone pattern. These should be angled downward.

SOIL AMENDMENTS

Chipped or composted bark Best used as a mulch

Composted manure Good all-around conditioner; must not contain weed seeds

Garden compost Good all-around amendment; must not contain weed seeds

Leaf mold Excellent conditioner and mulch

Peat Little nutrient value and breaks down too quickly to be of great value

Seaweed Excellent amendment because it includes plenty of minerals

Spent mushroom compost Good conditioner and mulch but includes lime

---

organic material

Organic material is important in all gardens as a soil amendment, as a nutrient for growing plants, and as a mulch to help preserve moisture and keep weeds down. The cheapest way to obtain it is to make your own compost by rotting down any weed-seed-free garden waste such as old herbaceous stems, flower heads, and grass clippings. Woody material will need to be shredded first. Any uncooked vegetable waste, such as peelings from the kitchen, can also be used. Make a compost bin, preferably with at least two sections. A similar bin should be used for composting fall leaves because leaf mold makes an excellent mulch. Composted manure is also a very useful addition to the soil as long as it does not contain weed seed.

compost bin
A compost bin should have at least two compartments: one for material that is rotting down, the other for collecting new material.

planting

Most climbers are sold in containers and can be planted at any time of the year, providing the weather is not too hot, cold, or dry and as long as they are kept watered and protected from strong winds. Bare-root plants or those being transplanted should be planted when temperatures will remain moderate as the new plants adjust: fall is best in the South, spring in the North. Prepare the hole with soil amendments to fit the plant; add slow-release granular fertilizer as well.

It is usually very dry next to a wall or fence, so plant climbers at least 12 in (30 cm) away from the boundary, using one or more canes to guide the stems into the wires or other support. Most climbing plants should be planted at the same depth as they were in their pots, indicated by the soil ring around the stem. The exception is clematis, which should be planted 2–3 in (5–7.5 cm) deeper.

Water the plant well and mulch with well-rotted organic material such as leaf mold or garden compost. Clematis like to have their roots cool so, if possible, either plant another shrub nearby to keep the sun off the soil around the roots or cover the ground with mulch, stone slabs or tile.

CLIMBERS

It is essential to understand the climbing and clinging method of a particular plant to know whether it will be successful in a given location. This knowledge will enable you to provide the most suitable support for the plant.

clinging: ivy
Clinging climbers need no additional support on a wall or fence as they creep up the structure, hugging close to the surface.

tendrils: clematis
Where tendrils are produced specifically for encircling a support, the plant will do well with a wire framework or climbing over another plant.

twining: honeysuckle
Plants that twine do best with a wire support or trellis. Growth can be assisted by directing shoots to a bare area of the support.

rambling: climbing roses
In the wild, such plants would ramble over trees and shrubs. They lean upon their support so, in cultivation, need to be tied to a structure.

PRUNING AND MAINTAINING CLIMBERS

maintenance

The sheer weight of an untended climber can damage a support, while overcrowding can adversely affect flower production. Pruning ensures an attractive framework and promotes vigorous growth and plentiful flowers. With these issues in mind, it is advisable to prune all climbing plants, even if it is only to cut out dead wood.

roses

Climbing and rambling roses can be very vigorous. They create excellent cover but benefit enormously from pruning and training. Unless you live in a mild-winter area, roses are best pruned in early spring, before new growth begins. Deadheading assists growth but should not be carried out if you want hips.

pruning a climbing rose
Do not prune during the first year. After that, only prune main shoots if they grow beyond their allotted space, but prune side shoots by two-thirds.

pruning a rambling rose
Do not prune during the first year. After that, remove two or three whole stems each year (it is easier to remove them in sections), and cut back the remaining main stems by a third and side shoots by two-thirds.

Despite the problem of thorns, untying roses from a wall, fence, or trellis and laying them on the ground makes pruning much easier. When all the unwanted material has been removed, the stems should be retrained onto the support—preferably in curving arches because this promotes flowering and presents a pleasing, open pattern.

clematis

Pruning clematis is a little complicated because different plants need different treatment. There are three groups and it is essential to know which group a specimen belongs to so you can prune correctly. The proper technique will encourage full growth and maximum flowering.

group 1

Early-flowering species that flower on the previous year's shoots: only prune out dead material. If you do not want the plant to become too large and heavy, remove a few older stems each year.

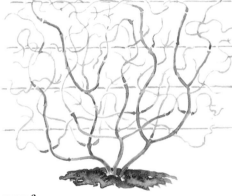

group 2

Large-flowered varieties that flower early to mid-season on new shoots from the previous year's stems: prune old wood lightly in early spring.

group 3

Large-flowered varieties that flower late on new wood: these can be cut right back, cutting just above a strong pair of buds. It looks brutal but they will grow all the stronger for this treatment. Prune in early spring.

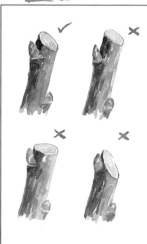

EXAMPLES OF CLEMATIS AND THEIR GROUP	
C. 'Abundance' 3	*C.* 'Jackmanii' 3
C. alpina 1	*C.* 'Lasurstern' 2
C. armandii 1	*C.* 'Little Nell' 3
C. 'Barbara Dibley' 2	*C. macropetala* 1
C. 'Barbara Jackman' 2	*C.* 'Marie Boisselot' 2
C. 'Bill MacKenzie' 3	*C.* 'Miss Bateman' 2
C. cirrhosa 1	*C. montana* 1
C. 'Comtesse de Bouchaud' 3	*C.* 'Mrs. Cholmondeley' 2
C. 'Countess of Lovelace' 2	*C.* 'Nelly Moser' 2
C. 'Daniel Deronda' 2	*C.* 'Niobe' 2
C. 'Doctor Ruppel' 2	*C.* 'Perle d'Azur' 3
C. 'Duchess of Albany' 3	*C.* 'Rouge Cardinal' 3
C. 'Elsa Späth' 2	*C.* 'Royal Velours' 3
C. 'Ernest Markham' 2	*C.* 'Star of India' 2
C. 'Etoile Violette' 3	*C. tangutica* 3
C. 'Gipsy Queen' 3	*C.* 'The President' 2
C. 'Hagley Hybrid' 3	*C. tibetana* 3
C. 'H. F. Young' 2	*C.* 'Ville de Lyon' 3
	C. viticella 3
	C. 'Vyvyan Pennell' 2
	C. 'W. E. Gladstone' 2

pruning cuts

Correct pruning cuts are very important to the health of all plants. Cuts should be sloping, just above a viable bud (above, top left).

wisteria

It is necessary to prune wisteria twice a year, once immediately after flowering and then again in the winter. Wisteria that is allowed to run free without any pruning soon runs out of flower-power. In midsummer, cut back all new growth to 6 in (15 cm) or four or five leaves. If you want to extend the plant's coverage, leave a few shoots to grow on. In early spring, reduce the stems even further to 3–4 in (7.5–10 cm) or two or three buds.

midsummer
Cut back all the new growth to 6 in (15 cm) or four or five leaves.

early spring
Cut back the stems even further than in summer, to 3–4 in (7.5–10 cm) or two or three buds.

other climbers

A simple pruning regime can make all the difference to the performance of a climber, but it is vital to know if the plant flowers on old or new wood. Follow these guidelines: remove all dead, diseased, and dying wood; cut out a few of the older stems to promote new, vigorous growth; do not allow plants to become tangled. Climbers that flower on old wood should be pruned immediately after flowering; those that flower on new wood should be left until late winter or spring.

plants that flower on new wood
Plants that flower on fresh growth should be pruned in late winter or early spring.

plants that flower on old wood
Plants that flower on the previous year's wood should be pruned directly after flowering. This will give them time to produce new shoots before winter.

ways of fixing plants to structures

A variety of devices and structures can be attached to walls and fences to give plants additional support. Wires can be discreet (see page 11 for attaching), wooden trellis is decorative, and for smaller areas and plants that produce good leaf cover, rigid plastic mesh is effective (although unattractive, which is why it needs to be hidden). For trellis, screw wood strips or blocks to the wall or fence (for brick walls, use masonry fasteners). These battens or blocks make it easier to weave stems behind the trellis and to tie them in. Plastic mesh is attached using clips that can be either screwed or nailed in place. The mesh can be unclipped to allow pruning or maintenance of the supporting structure.

wires
Vine eyes are hammered or screwed into walls and the wire is fed through and secured at the ends.

trellis
Wooden battens or blocks should be attached to the wall or fence and the trellis secured to these.

plastic mesh with clips
The clips are attached to the wall or fence and the mesh is held in place. The mesh can be unclipped for maintenance and access.

HEDGES
planting
Plant bare-root plants and those being transplanted when temperatures will remain moderate for them to adjust: fall is best in the South, spring in the North. Pot-grown plants can be planted at any time of the year as long as the weather is not extreme and the plants are kept watered. Mulch to preserve moisture and to keep weeds down; if necessary, protect with a windbreak.

maintenance
Formal hedges need regular clipping to keep them neat, but even this, in the case of slow-growing plants such as yew and boxwood,

only means once a year. Vigorous plants need clipping more often. Use a template and string (see page 45) to make sure the hedge is trimmed to a regular shape.

Informal hedges should be cut after flowering unless berries are required. They should be pruned rather than clipped, in the same way that you would prune a single shrub. There should be no attempt to cut them tight as you would with a formal hedge.

When clipping hedges, it can save a lot of time if you lay a large sheet on the ground to collect the trimmings. Do not leave clippings on the ground because grass and weeds will soon grow through them, making it difficult to remove both the clippings and the weeds. Shred and compost the pruned material and use it as a mulch and a soil amendment.

For good hedges, feed plants in the spring with a balanced slow-release fertilizer. There should be no need to water a hedge once it has become established.

TREES
Trees are frequently used along a boundary as a marker and to provide shelter and shade. Plant container-grown specimens at any time of year as long as the weather is not too extreme, but restrict the planting of bare-root trees to early spring.

Before planting, dig a large hole and hammer a stake into it. Plant the tree, spreading out the roots around the stake. The depth of the tree should be the same as it was in the pot or in the nursery bed, as indicated by the soil mark on the stem. Backfill the hole with good soil and pack it down. Use a tree-tie about 12 in (30 cm) above the soil to anchor the trunk to the stake. Keep watered until the tree has become established.

There is rarely a need to prune trees, other than fruit trees, except to remove dead or damaged branches, although it may be necessary to cut a tree back if it is getting too large or becoming misshapen.

staking trees
Anchor new trees with a tree-tie attached about 12 in (30 cm) from the ground.

WOODEN BOUNDARIES

Wood is a relatively cheap material for creating a boundary. It is very versatile, allowing for a wide range of shapes and styles, and generally not too difficult for the non-professional to use. Its life span is not as long as inert materials such as brick and stone but some types of lumber will last for many years, especially if regularly and thoroughly treated with preservative. Thin woods, particularly those covered with bark such as wattle hurdles, tend to last only a few years and should be considered as temporary fencing or screening.

choosing wood
Always choose the best quality wood you can afford. Hardwood lasts much longer than softwood but is expensive. If possible, choose the wood yourself rather than ordering it. Look for seasoned wood, preferably free from knots and other defects. Select lengths that are not warped or deformed. "Rough" (unplaned) timber is cheaper than "surfaced" (planed) wood and will do for many fencing and trellis projects, but its surface is rough, making it unsuitable for painting. Surfaced wood is smooth and is best for more refined structures and anything that needs a painted finish. Some lumberyards will cut and plane the wood to precisely the dimensions you require, which can save a lot of time and effort as well as provide a degree of accuracy that you might not be able to match.

preserving timber
It is possible to buy timber that has been treated with preservative. This is done under pressure, pushing the preservative much deeper into the grain of the wood than can be achieved by simply brushing it on. Treated wood is more expensive than untreated but the extra cost is worth it. All wooden structures should be treated every year with preservative. The best time to do this is during hot, dry weather when the wood is very porous and more likely to absorb the preservative. There are various preservatives available but avoid using the traditional creosote as this produces fumes that can have adverse effects on plants.

securing main posts
Whatever the quality of the wood and however well it has been preserved, if a fence or screen is not secured properly, it will be short-lived, particularly if it is in an exposed position or is carrying the weight of climbers or other plants. The main posts of any permanent structure, and even temporary screens that must withstand wind and weight, must be secured. As a rough guide, posts should be buried about half the exposed height of the post, or 6 in (150 mm) below the frost line in your area—whichever is greater. The hole should be about 4 in (10 cm) wider than the post. At the bottom of the hole plan to accommodate a 4-in (10-cm) layer of gravel, topped with a 6-in (15-cm) layer of concrete. Backfill with soil, packing it down with a tamper or a piece of lumber—unless the soil is loose or sandy, in which case backfill with concrete and use a concrete collar. Leave room at the top of the hole for a layer of soil and turf.

main-post foundations
Always secure the main posts of wooden structures with concrete on a gravel base.

joining timber
The better the fit of joints, the less chance there is of water getting in and starting rot. However, the quality of joinery and trellising, especially in rustic structures, is rarely as high in fencing as it is in other forms of carpentry and so lack of experience should not be a deterrent. In many cases, a simple butt joint with long galvanized nails holding the two pieces of wood together is sufficient. Always use galvanized nails as ordinary steel nails rapidly corrode and work loose.

Properly made joints, however, are stronger and will last longer. These need not be the complicated dovetail joints of cabinetmaking; simple halved joints are among the most useful. Here, a section of wood, half the thickness of the piece of wood, is removed from each piece so that the two nestle together. The pieces of wood can be in a straight line, at right angles, or at a more oblique angle—the principle is the same in each case. Secure the joint with galvanized nails for most fencing but, for more sophisticated work, use glue and wooden dowels.

When hammering a nail into trelliswork or any structure that is not solid or is not lying flat on the ground, hold a heavy hammer on the opposite side of the wood to absorb the impact of the blow. This makes the job much easier.

butt joints

Butt joints are versatile, effective, and straightforward to make. Simply abut the two pieces of wood so that they sit neatly together, and secure with a long galvanized nail. The result is surprisingly solid.

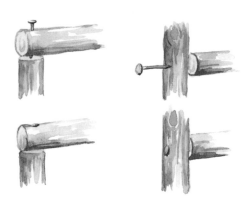

butt joints
The simplest joint, two pieces of wood are secured by a galvanized nail. No shaping is needed.

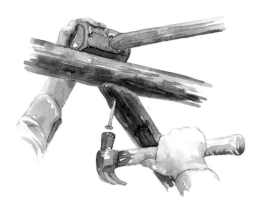

using a sledgehammer
When hammering a nail into a structure that is not on the ground, a hammer held on the opposite side of the wood will give stability.

birds-mouth joint
This simple joint comprises a niche removed from one piece of wood and a corresponding carved end in the other. Secure with galvanized nails.

halved joints

More complicated than butt joints, halved joints involve the removal of a section of wood from each of two pieces to be joined, cutting the same sized niche into half the thickness of each piece.

cutting a half-joint
Wedge the piece of wood so that it is firm, and slice out the joint using a chisel and hammer.

fitting a half-joint
Fit the two pieces together, adjusting as necessary, and secure them with a galvanized nail.

joints with dowels and glue

For a more professional finish, a wooden dowel should be used. Carve the joint and drill holes that will allow the dowel to fit tightly. Glue and secure with the dowel.

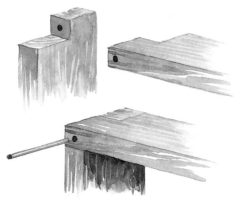

right-angle joints using a wooden dowel
A right-angle joint secured with a half joint, glue, and dowel is solid and neat in appearance.

cross-joints using a wooden dowel
A cross-shaped fixture can also be held together with glue and a dowel.

SOLID BOUNDARIES

Although the materials are expensive, brick and stone walls can be long lasting and provide an ideal home for many climbing and tender plants. Walls must be well made, so if you doubt your ability to build a secure, safe structure, hire a professional. However, two or three courses (layers) of bricks or walls up to 18 in (45 cm) high should be within the ability of most gardeners.

foundations
On heavier soils, walls up to 2 ft (60 cm) high need footings of 4 in (10 cm) of well-packed broken rocks and 6 in (15 cm) of concrete. Higher walls need 4 in (10 cm) of broken rocks and 10 in (25 cm) of concrete. On softer ground the depth of concrete should be doubled. If in doubt, consult a professional. Foundations should be at least 2 in (5 cm) wider on each side than the width of the wall, and the top of the concrete should lie 2 in (5 cm) below the level of the ground to allow a recess for the first brick or stone. In areas that have frost in winter, the foundation should be 6 in (15 cm) below the frost line in the area. Foundations on sloping ground should be stepped and not run parallel to the ground.

basic foundations
Broken rocks and concrete should be used in well-calculated proportions for successful foundations.

foundations on a slope
Stepped foundations must be used on a slope to give a solid finish to a wall .

mixing concrete
You can buy concrete as a ready-to-use mix (just add water) or mix it yourself. Although it is more expensive, the ready-to-use concrete is easier, especially if you need less than 1 cu yd (1 cu m). An 80-lb bag of mix makes about ⅔ cu ft. You can mix one bag at a time in a garden wheelbarrow. If you want to make your own, the ratios are as follows: 1 part portland cement, 2.5 parts sand,

2.5 parts gravel and 0.5 parts water. Keep in mind that the amount of water can vary quite a bit—add only a small amount at a time. The easiest method is to use a mixing drum or a rented concrete mixer. Add water a little at a time until the mixture is of the right consistency. Avoid making it too wet (see step 3). To make concrete by hand, follow the instructions below.

hand-mixing concrete
1 *Place the concrete mix or dry ingredients on a large board. Mound it in the center of the board and make a crater in the center of the mound.*

2 *A little at a time, pour water into the crater; it should not run out of the crater.*

3 *Mix the concrete and the water, and add more water if necessary.*

To test for the correct consistency, slice the mixed concrete with a spade. The edges should hold straight. If the edges crumble, add more water. If the edges fall over, add more dry ingredients.

mortar

You can buy pre-mixed mortar or make your own to the following ratios: 1 part portland cement, 1 part hydrated lime, 6 parts sand. The mixture should have the consistency of soft butter. Adding a little liquid soap to the mix makes it more plastic and easier to use.

Flemish bond
Two bricks deep, this pattern has one, three, or five stretchers to one header per layer.

making mortar
Mortar needs the easy-spread consistency of soft butter. A little liquid soap can help.

brick walls

Walls should usually be at least two bricks wide, that is 9 in (23 cm), although a single width of bricks can be used for walls of only two or three layers (or courses). The pattern that bricks make is important for strength as well as appearance. The common patterns (or bonds) are English bond and Flemish bond (both two-bricks thick) and running bond (a single-brick thickness).

running bond
A single brick deep, this bond comprises only stretchers. These must be laid in a staggered formation for maximum strength.

English bond
Two bricks deep, this pattern comprises several layers of stretchers (long-side out)—one, three, or five—to one layer of headers (short-end out).

check level top and side
It is essential that walls are level in all directions, and a level should be used constantly as the wall is built. Build the ends first and, using a line as a guide, build the center one row at a time.

raised beds

Raised beds can be an enormous asset in a garden, particularly where space is limited. They are very effective in small town gardens, where they complement the adjacent house. Low structures, they are ideal for a novice builder. Raised beds of brick, stone, or concrete blocks require foundations. To provide drainage, leave gaps in the vertical pointing in the lower courses of the brickwork.

To prepare the bed, put a layer of broken rocks in the base and fill with good soil and organic material.

joining one wall to another

If joining a new wall to an existing one, the new wall can be keyed into the old one. Cut out bricks from every other course of the existing wall and insert bricks from the new wall. Alternatively, use wall ties that will firmly secure one wall into the other. Ties are available from building suppliers and come in many forms. Follow the instructions supplied. Both methods apply to straight walls and right angles.

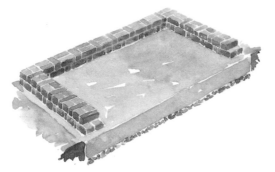

foundations
Create foundations of gravel and concrete, then build the raised bed, one course at a time. Larger beds need a two-brick-deep bond.

joining on a straight wall
Where an existing wall is being extended, neatly cut a brick out from every other course to form a toothed surface. Insert bricks from the new wall.

drainage
Drainage is provided by means of broken stones in the base and sand added to the soil and well-rotted organic material.

joining at right angles
1 *Carefully remove a brick from alternate course of bricks. These can be worked loose by chipping the mortar away.*

other materials
Railroad ties do not need foundations. Lay them on a flat base and stagger the corner joints, leaving small gaps for drainage.

2 *Build the new wall into the niches, using the same bond as in the original wall and a level to make sure the surfaces are straight.*

useful addresses

NURSERIES AND PLANT SPECIALISTS

Avant Gardens
710 High Hill Road
North Dartmouth
MA 02747-1363
(508) 998-8819
www.avantgardensNE.com
Uncommon plants, including tender perennials and alpines.

Bamboo Sourcery
666 Wagnon Road
Sebastapol, CA 95472
(707) 823-5866
www.bamboosourcery.com
A wide choice of bamboo.

Bluestone Perennials
7211 Middle Ridge Road
Madison, OH 44057-3096
(800) 852-5243
www.bluestoneperennials.com
Perennials, plants, herbs, ornamental shrubs, and bulbs.

The Cook's Garden
P.O. Box 5010
Hodges, SC 29653-5010
Seeds for herbs, vegetables, flowers.

Dutch Gardens
P.O. Box 2037
Lakewood, NJ 08701
www.dutchgardens.com
Holland's finest bulbs.

Eastern Plant Specialties
Box 5692
Clark, NJ 07066
(732) 382-2508
www.easternplant.com
Special emphasis on native and woodland plants.

Glasshouse Works
P.O. Box 97
Church Street
Stewart, OH 45778-0097
(800) 837-2142
www.rareplants.com
Tropicals, perennials, herbs, and annuals. Coleus is a specialty.

Heronswood Nursery
7530 NE 288th Street
Kingston, WA 98346
(360) 297-4172
www.heronswood.com
Perennials, annuals, herbs, trees, and shrubs, for collectors and connoisseurs.

Johnny's Selected Seeds
Foss Hill Road
RR 1 Box 2580
Albion, ME 04910
(207) 437-4301
www.johnnyseeds.com
All the basics, plus many unusual varieties.

Lilypons Water Gardens
6800 Lilypons Lane
P.O. Box 10
Buckeystown, MD 21717
www.lilypons.com
Water-gardening supplies, as well as tropical lilies and lotus.

McClure & Zimmerman
108 W. Winnebago
P.O. Box 368
Friesland, WI 53935-0368
800-883-6998
www.mzbulb.com
Not just autumn bulbs, but many of the summer bloomers, including flowering onions.

Miller Nurseries
5060 West Lake Road
Canandaigua, NY 14424
Grape specialists, but also plenty of other fruit trees and shrubs.

New England Bamboo Co.
5 Granite Street
Rockport, MA 01966
www.newengbamboo.com
Bamboo and a wonderful selection of ornamental grasses.

Plant Delights Nursery
9241 Sauls Road
Raleigh, NC 27603
(919) 772-4794
www.plantdelights.com
An amazing selection of hostas. Plus cannas, callas and other tropicals, and aquatic plants.

Select Seeds
180 Stickney Hill Road
Union, CT 06076
(860) 684-9310
www.selectseeds.com
The focus here is on heirloom seeds, but plants are offered, too.

Shepherd's Garden Seeds
30 Irene Street
Torrington, CT 06790
(860) 482-0532
www.shepherdseeds.com
Seeds, annuals, perennials, vegetables, herbs, and some fruit.

Stokes
P.O. Box 548
Buffalo, NY 14240
(800) 396-9238
www.stokeseeds.com
Vegetables, seeds, annuals, perennials, herbs, some bulbs.

The Thyme Garden
20546 Alsea Highway
Alsea, OR 97324
(541) 487-8671
www.thymegarden.com
*Sixty varieties of thyme, and
hundreds of other plants.*

Waterford Gardens
74 East Allendale Road
Saddle River, NJ 07458.
(201) 327-0721
www.waterfordgardens.com
Pond supplies, plants, and fish.

Wayside Gardens
Garden Lane
Hodges, SC 29695-0001
(800) 845-1124
www.waysidegardens.com
Plants, perennials, and flowers.

We-Du Nurseries
2055 Polly Spout Road
Marion, NC 28752
(828)738-8300
*Perennials, wildflowers, shrubs,
trees, bulbs, aquatic plants.*

White Flower Farm
P.O. Box 50
Litchfield, CT 06759
(800) 503-9624
www.whiteflowerfarm.com
*Perennials, annuals, and
some shrubs.*

**PLANTERS AND
GARDEN STRUCTURES**

Charleston Gardens
61 Queen Street
Charleston, SC 29401
(800) 469-0118
www.charlestongardens.com
*Planters and jardinieres; lighting,
garden features, fountains.*

Florentine Craftsmen
46-24 28th Street
Long Island City, NY 11101
(718) 937-7632
www.florentinecraftsmen.com
*Classic furniture, fountains,
statuary, planters, and urns.*

Gardener's Supply Company
128 Intervale Road
Burlington, VT 05401
*Lightweight planters, as well as
obelisks, willow fences and
borders, trellises, and statuary.*

Martha by Mail
P.O. Box 60060
Tampa, FL 33660
(800) 950-7130
www.marthabymail.com
Classy containers and ornaments.

Seibert & Rice
P.O. Box 365
Short Hills, NJ 07078
(973) 467-8266
www.seibert-rice.com
*Exquisite terra-cotta, pots,
troughs, and urns.*

Smith & Hawken
35 Corte Madera Avenue
Mill Valley, CA 94941
(800) 940-1170
www.smith-hawken.com
Simple and classic containers.

Stone Forest
P.O. Box 2840
Santa Fe NM, 87504
(505) 986-8883
www.stoneforest.com
*Hand-carved granite sculpture in
Japanese and contemporary styles;
basins, fountains, functional
sculpture, and stepping stones.*

Trellis Structures
60 River Street
Beverly, MA 01915
(888) 285-4624
www.trellisstructures.com
*Arbors and trellises from
traditional to contemporary;
pergolas, chairs, and benches.*

Vermont Outdoor Furniture
9 Auburn Street
Barre, VT 05641
(800) 588-8834
*Simple, beautiful wooden
benches, chairs, porch swings,
gliders, and tables.*

Walt Nicke's Garden Talk
P.O. Box 433
Topsfield, MA 01983
(978) 887-3388
www.gardentalk.com
*Arches, obelisks and gazebos; fine
tools and garden ornaments.*

Wood Classics
20 Osprey Lane
Gardiner, NY 12525
(845) 255-7871
*Elegant, simple wood furniture:
chairs, benches, gliders,
umbrellas, and tables.*

**LUMBER AND
BUILDING SUPPLIES**

Ace Hardware Corporation
Stores nationwide
(630) 990-6600
www.acehardware.com

The Home Depot
Stores nationwide
(800) 430-3376
www.homedepot.com
*Bricks, pavers, stone, lumber
and hardware.*

credits

The publishers would like to thank the following illustrators for their contribution to the book: Martine Collings, David Atkinson, Lizzie Saunders, Amanda Patton, and Anne Winterbotham. They would also like to thank the owners of the following gardens for their help:

Axletree Garden and Nursery, Peasmarch, East Sussex; Bates Green, Arlington, East Sussex; Beth Chatto Gardens, Elmstead Market, Essex; Cinque Cottage, Ticehurst, East Sussex; Grace Barrand Design Centre, Nutfield, Surrey; Hadspen Garden and Nursery, Castle Cary, Somerset; Hailsham Grange, Hailsham, East Sussex; Holkham Gardens, Wells-next-the-Sea, Norfolk; King John's Lodge, Etchingham, East Sussex; Marle Place, Brenchley, Kent; Sue Martin, Frittenden, Kent; Merriments Garden, Hurst Green, East Sussex; Queen Anne's, Goudhurst, Kent; Rogers Rough, Kilndown, Kent; Snape Cottage, Chaffeymoor, Dorset; Sticky Wicket Garden, Buckland Newton, Dorset; Upper Mill Cottage, Loose, Kent; Wyland Wood, Robertsbridge, East Sussex

All the photographs in this book were taken by Stephen Robson except for those on the following pages, which are courtesy of Jerry Harpur: 66, 69, 92, and 95.

index

acknowledgments

The author would like to thank all those involved in bringing this
book to fruition: Anne Ryland whose idea it was and who
commissioned me to write it; Sarah Polden for her editing as well as
her many suggestions; Mark Latter and Liz Brown for their brilliant
design work; and all the illustrators for the hours they spent turning
my rough sketches into something worth looking at.

Thanks also to all the owners who allowed us to photograph their
beautiful gardens for the book.

fences *and* hedges